Air Fryer Cookbook For Beginners

by Karen Klock

Table of Contents

Introduction

Do you have an Air Fryer but don't know how to make the most out of it? Don't worry! In this Air Fryer Cookbook, you'll learn to cook healthy and tasty meals without using too much oil and fat, or effort for that matter. This recipe collection has everything you need, from French fries and meats to vegan meals and amazing appetizers, and even some yummy desserts. If you are starting a new diet, the air fryer can be your new best friend. It opens a whole new world of cooking possibilities.

The recipes in this book can be used with any air fryer model. In addition, you can modify the recipes by adjusting their time, temperature, or quantity of ingredients - if you want to cook for more or fewer people. With this kitchen device, you can prepare flavorful and crispy food, and you will be pleasantly surprised by the low number of calories and the awesome taste.

I am sure you will love this book, whether you are new to the air fryer world or even if you are an experienced air fryer master in the kitchen you can still learn a thing or two.

What is an Air Fryer?

An Air Fryer is a modern kitchen appliance similar to a convection oven. It can roast and bake dishes with little or no oil. Food comes out very crunchy and delicious thanks to the rapid circulation of hot air. Air-fried food is a healthy alternative to deep-fried foods but with lower content of fat and calories.

Air Fryers usually have a digital screen and touch panel, allowing you to set the time and temperature easily. The time and temperature usually vary from 5 to 25 minutes and 350° to 400°F. Each program you select will suggest a time and temperature setting or you can adjust them manually depending on the recipe's recommendation. During cooking, it may be necessary to flip or turn the food halfway through the cooking time to help it crisp up evenly.

Your air fryer may come with different accessories such as a grill rack, cupcake pan, mesh basket, etc. In addition, there are many other air fryer accessories on the market. For instance - grill pans, pizza pans, basket dividers, baking inserts, etc. They are versatile and comfortable for preparing delicious meals, so getting a few of them might be a good idea for you.

How to Use Your Air Fryer with This Cookbook?

Six steps to get the best from your air fryer:

- **Select a recipe -** choose a recipe that is suitable to cook in your air fryer.
- **Prepare all the ingredients -** collect all the ingredients you need and prepare the meal according to the instructions.
- **Prepare your Air Fryer –** prepare any accessories that you might need like - muffin pans, rotisserie, cake pans, basket, or rack. Make sure these accessories fit properly in your air fryer.
- **Avoid overcrowding -** it is better to cook in small batches because this will allow the air to circulate more efficiently and cook the food better.
- **Keep an eye on the food - during** the cooking, **it** is best to open the air fryer and shake the basket in order to promote even cooking.
- **Use cooking spray -** don't forget to use at least a little bit of cooking spray or oil. Otherwise, you risk having your food stuck to the basket.

Benefits of the Air Fryer

Here are a few benefits of using an air fryer:

- **Healthy -** Air Fryer needs much smaller amounts of oil compared to conventional cooking, as a result Air-Fried food will have fewer calories.
- **Quick meals -** When you are busy, this is your best option. The Air Fryer can cook delicious meals much faster than an oven. That means you shouldn't spend a tremendous amount of time in the kitchen.
- **Easy to clean -** The basket and all other accessories are removable. You can wash them in a dishwasher or with a sponge and soap. Always wait for the Air Fryer to cool down and then start with the cleaning to avoid burning yourself.
- **Energy effective -** If you want to preheat your Air Fryer, it will only take a few minutes (2-4 minutes), which is more effective than heating the oven (10-15minutes).

Air Fryer FAQ

Here I will share with you the answers to the frequently asked questions about the Air Fryer:

1. **What can I cook in the Air fryer?** You can cook almost everything from vegetables, meats, snacks, beans, frozen foods, fries to muffins and cakes. The list is so extensive.

2. **Is Air-fryer food healthy?** Yes, it is a healthy cooking method because you are cooking with less oil while maintaining most of the taste from traditional frying.

3. **Should I put oil in the Air Fryer?** Yes, you should. You need to use one tablespoon of oil (vegetable oil, olive oil, peanut oil, canola oil) or cooking spray applied to the basket or the food itself. Even if you don't use oil it is not a huge problem. Just shake a few times while cooking to avoid sticking.

4. **Should I preheat my Air Fryer?** You don't need to preheat your Air Fryer. The total time it took to cook a meal in a hot air fryer was the same as when we cooked food in a cold Air Fryer.

5. **How much food can I prepare in Air Fryer?** You can prepare food for 2 to 4 servings but don't over-crowd the basket. When you want to cook more food, work in batches and check for doneness earlier.

6. **Is the Air Fryer worth it?** Of course! It is fast, delicious, and saves space on the countertop. You will be satisfied with the results.

7. **Are Air Fryers toxic?** Air Fryers are not harmful. You need to know how to use it and follow all the manufacturer's instructions and guidelines.

8. **Is air-fried food crispy?** Yes! Air Fryer makes perfect crunchy food. It would be best to be informed how to use the different settings correctly to achieve the desired result.

1. Sweet Potato Sticks with Dipping Sauce

4 Servings   25 minutes

Ingredients

- 1 teaspoon salt
- 1/2 teaspoon chili powder
- 1/2 teaspoon black pepper
- 1 tablespoon fresh rosemary, finely chopped
- 1/3 teaspoon smoked paprika
- 1 ½ lb. sweet potatoes, peeled and sliced into ½ inch sticks
- 1 ½ tablespoon olive oil
- For the Dipping Sauce:
- 1/2 cup mayonnaise
- 1/2 cup yogurt
- ½ teaspoon garlic powder
- ½ teaspoon fresh lemon juice
- 1 tablespoon fresh dill, chopped

Directions

Add the sliced sweet potatoes to a large bowl. Stir in the olive oil, salt, pepper, rosemary, chili powder, and smoked paprika. Mix well.

Add the potatoes to the preheated Air Fryer and cook for 19 minutes at 360 degrees F, shaking the basket halfway through the cooking time.

Meanwhile, in a small bowl combine well the yogurt, mayonnaise, lemon juice, fresh dill, and garlic powder.

Serve the potato sticks warm with the dipping sauce on the side. Enjoy!

Nutritional Information

Calories 302; Fat 7g; Carbs 46.4g; Fiber 7.3g; Protein 3.7g

2. Sautéed Green Beans

2 Servings   15 minutes

Ingredients

- 1/2 teaspoon salt
- 1/2 tablespoon balsamic vinegar
- 1 ½ tablespoon soy sauce
- 1/2 teaspoon pepper
- 1 lb. green beans, cleaned
- ½ teaspoon garlic powder
- 1 ½ tablespoon sesame oil
- 1 tablespoon sesame seeds

Directions

In a large bowl add the green beans, soy sauce, vinegar, salt, pepper, sesame oil, and garlic powder. Mix well and let them marinate for 15 minutes

Place the green beans into the preheated Air Fryer. Cook for 10 minutes at 390 degrees F shaking the basket halfway through the cooking time.

Serve the green beans warm and sprinkle with sesame seeds. Bon appétit!

Nutritional Information

Calories 237; Fat 12.9g; Carbs 28.9g; Fiber 8g; Protein 6.2g

3. Stuffed Potatoes with Bacon

4 Servings   35 minutes

Ingredients

- 1/2 cup cheddar cheese, shredded
- 2 tablespoons fresh chives, chopped
- 3 slices bacon, diced
- 4 medium potatoes
- 1 tablespoon fresh coriander, minced
- 1 tablespoon olive oil
- 1/2 teaspoon salt
- 1/2 teaspoon pepper

Directions

First, prick your potatoes with a small paring knife. Place them in the preheated Air Fryer for 22 minutes at 380 degrees F or until cooked through.

Meanwhile, add the olive oil to a skillet and stir in the onion and bacon. Cook for 5-6 minutes or until the bacon is brown. Set aside.

When your potatoes are cooked, open them up with a knife. Stuff the potatoes with the cooked bacon, onion, cheddar cheese, and coriander.

Return the potatoes to the Air Fryer for 3-4 minutes or until the cheese is melted. Serve and sprinkle with fresh chives. Enjoy!

Nutritional Information

Calories 338; Fat 16g; Carbs 39.4g; Fiber 2.8g; Protein 10.6g

4. Classic Brussels Sprouts

3 Servings   20 minutes

Ingredients

- ½ teaspoon dried thyme
- 1 ½ lb. Brussels sprouts
- 1/2 teaspoon pepper
- 1 tablespoon canola oil
- ½ teaspoon dried coriander
- ½ teaspoon salt
- 1 teaspoon paprika

Directions

In a large bowl place the Brussels sprouts and toss with canola oil, dried coriander, paprika, pepper, salt, and thyme. Combine well.

Then, place the Brussels sprouts in the preheated Air Fryer for 18 minutes at 390 degrees F, shaking the basket halfway through the cooking time.

Serve warm immediately and enjoy. Bon appétit!

Nutritional Information

Calories 172; Fat 8.3g; Carbs 21.3g; Fiber 7.2g; Protein 5.1g

5. Stuffed Mushrooms with Cheese

3 Servings   15 minutes

Ingredients

- 1 tablespoon fresh coriander, chopped
- 12 medium-sized mushrooms, cut off the stems
- 2 tablespoons cheddar cheese, shredded
- 1/2 teaspoon pepper
- 2 tablespoons melted butter
- 3 tablespoons parmesan, shredded
- 1/3 cup breadcrumbs
- 2 cloves garlic, pressed
- 1/2 teaspoon salt

Directions

In a bowl add the breadcrumbs, melted butter, parmesan cheese, salt, cheddar cheese, pepper, and fresh coriander. Mix well.

Stuff the mushroom caps with the cheese filling. Then, place the mushrooms in the preheated Air Fryer and cook at 370 degrees F for 10 minutes or until cooked through.

Serve immediately and enjoy!

Nutritional Information

Calories 201; Fat 10g; Carbs 16.3g; Fiber 4.1g; Protein 8.3g

6. Marinated Chicken Breasts

2 Servings   20 minutes

Ingredients

- 1/3 cup of mayonnaise
- ½ teaspoon dried oregano
- 1/2 teaspoon turmeric powder
- 2 tablespoons chili sauce
- 1/2 teaspoon brown sugar
- ½ teaspoon garlic powder
- 1 teaspoon salt
- 2 tablespoons Dijon mustard
- 1/2 teaspoon pepper
- 2 chicken breasts
- ½ teaspoon dried basil

Directions

In a large mixing bowl combine the oregano, garlic powder, basil, mustard, brown sugar, mayonnaise, chili sauce, salt, pepper, and turmeric.

Add the chicken breasts to the mixing bowl and cover with foil. Let it marinate for at least 3-4 hours in your fridge.

Remove the chicken from the marinade. Then, place the chicken in the Air Fryer basket and cook for 20 minutes or until cooked through.

Serve warm and enjoy!

Nutritional Information

Calories 478; Fat 29g; Carbs 7.3g; Fiber 2.2g; Protein 37.9g

7. Tender Chicken Legs

3 Servings | 25 minutes + marinating time

Ingredients

- 3 large chicken legs
- 1 ½ tablespoon canola oil
- ½ teaspoon pepper
- 1/3 cup of honey
- 1 tablespoon lemon juice
- ½ cup of dry white wine
- 1/2 cup of soy sauce
- ½ teaspoon paprika
- 1 tablespoon Worcestershire sauce
- ½ teaspoon salt

Directions

In a large bowl mix the canola oil, white wine, honey, lemon juice, salt, pepper, soy sauce, paprika, and Worcestershire sauce.

Then add the chicken legs to the marinade. Marinate for 30 minutes in your refrigerator.

Place the chicken legs in the preheated Air Fryer and cook for 22 minutes at 390 degrees F, turning them over once or twice to ensure even cooking.

Serve the chicken legs warm with your favorite side dish.

Nutritional Information

Calories 498; Fat 17.2g; Carbs 8.5g; Fiber 0.3g; Protein 38.6g

8. Stuffed Chicken Breast with Cheddar

4 Servings   20 minutes

Ingredients

- 4 small-sized chicken breasts, bone-less and skinless
- 1/4 cup pizza sauce
- 1/2 cup Cheddar cheese, shredded
- 4 slices ham
- Salt and pepper, to taste
- 1 ½ tablespoon olive oil
- 1 tablespoon dried basil

Directions

Carefully flatten out the chicken breasts using a rolling pin.

Brush them with olive oil, then, divide the ham, basil, sauce, and cheddar cheese among the four chicken breasts.

Roll the chicken fillets with the stuffing inside and seal them using two toothpicks.

Roast in the preheated Air Fryer for 15 minutes at 380 degrees F or until thoroughly cooked.

Bon appétit!

Nutritional Information

Calories 513; Fat 21g; Carbs 7.5g; Fiber 0.2g; Protein 76.6g

9. Chicken Meatballs

4 Servings   15 minutes

Ingredients

- 1 lb. ground chicken
- 1 onion, finely chopped
- 2 cloves garlic, minced
- 2 tablespoons canola oil
- ½ teaspoon salt
- ½ teaspoon pepper
- 1/4 cup grated Pecorino Romano
- 4 tablespoons breadcrumbs
- 1/2 teaspoon cumin powder

Directions

Place the ground chicken, onion, minced garlic, breadcrumbs, salt, pepper, cumin, and cheese in a mixing dish and stir until everything is well incorporated.

Use an ice cream scoop to shape the meat into golf ball-sized meatballs.

Then, place the meatballs in a single layer in the preheated Air Fryer at 380 degrees F for 10 minutes or until cooked through. Work in batches.

Serve warm! Bon appétit!

Nutritional Information

Calories 261; Fat 16.8g; Carbs 7g; Fiber 0.9g; Protein 21.1g

10. Crispy Chicken Fingers

4 Servings   20 minutes

Ingredients

- ½ teaspoon onion powder
- 1 lb. chicken tenderloins, cut into chunks
- 1/2 cup all-purpose flour
- ½ teaspoon paprika
- ½ teaspoon salt
- 1 tablespoon Dijon mustard
- 1 ½ cups milk
- ½ teaspoon pepper
- 1/2 cup cornmeal mix
- 1 teaspoon oregano
- ½ teaspoon thyme

Directions

Grab two bowls. In the first bowl, combine the cornmeal, onion powder, salt, pepper, paprika, flour, oregano, and thyme. Mix the mustard and milk in the second one.

Then, dip each strip into the milk mixture and after that, cover them with the cornmeal mixture on all sides.

Transfer the prepared chicken fingers to the preheated Air Fryer and cook for 13 minutes at 370 degrees F.

Serve with your favorite dipping sauce and enjoy!

Nutritional Information

Calories 498; Fat 17.2g; Carbs 8.5g; Fiber 0.3g; Protein 38.6g

11. Aromatic Turkey Skewers

4 Servings 20 minutes

Ingredients

- 1 lb. turkey chunks
- 2 red bell peppers, sliced
- 3 tablespoons vegetable oil
- 2 tablespoons fresh parsley, finely chopped
- 3/4 teaspoon salt
- 1 tablespoon fresh rosemary, finely chopped
- ½ teaspoon paprika
- ½ teaspoon garlic powder
- 2 tablespoons fresh lemon juice

Directions

Soak wooden skewers in water for 40 minutes.

Then, place the vegetable oil, turkey chunks, paprika, salt, parsley, rosemary, lemon juice, and garlic powder in a large bowl. Coat well and marinate for 1 hour in the refrigerator.

Thread the meat, green pepper, onion, and yellow pepper onto the skewers.

Cook the skewers in the preheated Air Fryer for 15 minutes, turning them over once or twice to ensure even cooking.

Serve immediately with your favorite dipping sauce.

Nutritional Information

Calories 256; Fat 12.6g; Carbs 8.8g; Fiber 1.3g; Protein 26.9g

12. Eye-Catching Turkey Meatballs

3 Servings   20 minutes

Ingredients

- 1 lb. ground turkey
- 1 teaspoon dried oregano
- ½ teaspoon dried basil
- ½ cup breadcrumbs
- 1 egg, whisked
- 1 green onion,
- 2 garlic cloves, minced
- 1 teaspoon red pepper flakes
- 1/4 cup olive oil
- 3/4 teaspoon salt
- 1/4 cup grated Pecorino Romano

Directions

In a large bowl place all of the above ingredients and mix until everything is well incorporated.

Shape the mixture into balls. Then, place the meatballs into the preheated Air Fryer and cook for 13 minutes at 390 degrees F or until cooked through. Work in batches.

Serve with your favorite sauce. Bon appétit!

Nutritional Information

Calories 413; Fat 31.2g; Carbs 2.5g; Fiber 0.7g; Protein 32g

13. Turkey Tenderloins

3 Servings 45 minutes

Ingredients

- 1/2 teaspoon dried marjoram
- 2 tablespoons fresh coriander, minced
- 1lb. turkey breasts
- 3 tablespoons sesame oil
- ½ teaspoon pepper
- ½ teaspoon salt
- 2 tablespoons dry white wine
- 1 tablespoon fresh thyme, finely chopped
- 1 tablespoon fresh sage, finely chopped

Directions

In a large bowl stir in the turkey breast, marjoram, sesame oil, fresh coriander, salt, pepper, white wine, fresh thyme, and fresh sage. Mix well until the turkey breasts are coated well on all sides.

Cook the turkey breasts in the preheated Air Fryer at 370 degrees F for 25 minutes or until cooked through. Work in batches, if necessary.

Leave to rest for 10 minutes and slice. Serve and enjoy!

Nutritional Information

Calories 393; Fat 24.4g; Carbs 7.6g; Fiber 0.7g; Protein 33.7g

14. Stuffed Zucchini with Ground Turkey

3 Servings   30 minutes

Ingredients

- 1/4 cup olive oil
- ½ lb. ground turkey
- 1 yellow onion, finely chopped
- 2 cloves garlic, minced
- 1 tablespoon fresh cilantro, chopped
- 1 tablespoon fresh parsley, chopped
- 3 tablespoons chopped tomatoes
- Salt and black pepper, to taste
- 4 medium zucchini
- 1/3 cup parmesan cheese, shredded

Directions

Slice the zucchini into halves. Then, with a spoon scoop out the flesh. Slice the flesh and reserve.

In a large pan, heat the olive oil, then add the onion, garlic, ground turkey, and cook for 4 minutes.

Stir in the reserved zucchini flesh, tomato sauce, cilantro, parsley, salt, and pepper. Cook for 2-3 minutes more.

Spoon the mixture into the zucchini. Transfer them to the preheated Air Fryer.

Cook at 370 degrees F for 16 minutes. Then, top with parmesan cheese. Cook for 1-2 minutes more or until the cheese is melted.

Serve immediately and enjoy!

Nutritional Information

Calories 471; Fat 36.4g; Carbs 11.4g; Fiber 1.3g; Protein 25.8g

15. Spicy Turkey Wings

2 Servings   20 minutes

Ingredients

- 1 lb. turkey wings, cut into pieces
- 1 teaspoon garlic powder
- 1/2 teaspoon paprika
- ½ teaspoon chili powder
- 2 tablespoons soy sauce
- 3 tablespoons Tabasco sauce
- ½ teaspoon cumin
- 2 tablespoons fresh lemon juice
- ½ teaspoon Kosher salt
- ½ teaspoon pepper
- 1/4 cup olive oil

Directions

In a large saucepan with boiling water, add the turkey wings and boil for 18 minutes.

Then, in a mixing bowl add the turkey wings, garlic powder, paprika, salt, pepper, chili powder, soy sauce, Tabasco sauce, cumin, lemon juice, and olive oil. Mix well.

Air-fry the wings for 15 minutes at 380 degrees F in the preheated Air Fryer, turning them over once or twice to ensure even cooking.

Serve immediately and enjoy!

Nutritional Information

Calories 490; Fat 31.4g; Carbs 7.2g; Fiber 1.1g; Protein 47.8g

16. Aromatic Pork Chops

Ingredients

- 2 pork chops
- 1 teaspoon onion powder
- 1/2 teaspoon garlic powder
- 1 tablespoon brown sugar
- Salt and pepper, to taste
- 1 teaspoon paprika
- 1 tablespoon mustard
- 2 tablespoons soy sauce
- 1 teaspoon dried cilantro
- 2 tablespoons olive oil

Directions

Add the pork chops, olive oil, garlic powder, onion powder, brown sugar, paprika, mustard, soy sauce, dried cilantro, salt, and pepper into a zip-top plastic bag. Shake up to coat well.

Then, transfer the pork chops to the preheated Air Fryer. Air fry them for 15 minutes at 390 degrees F.

Serve warm with your favorite side dish. Bon appétit!

Nutritional Information

Calories 312; Fat 9.9g; Carbs 12.8g; Fiber 1.7g; Protein 41.3g

17. Tender Pork Ribs

4 Servings | 25 minutes + marinating time

Ingredients

- 1 lb. baby back ribs
- 3 tablespoons olive oil
- 1/2 teaspoon pepper
- 1/2 teaspoon smoked salt
- 1 tablespoon Dijon mustard
- 1/3 cup soy sauce
- 2 cloves garlic, minced
- 1/2 cup BBQ sauce

Directions

First, remove the membrane from the back of the ribs. Cut them in half so it will be easy to fit in the Air Fryer.

Place the olive oil, pepper, salt, Dijon mustard, soy sauce, garlic, and baby back ribs in a large-sized mixing dish. Cover and marinate in your refrigerator for 2 hours.

Add the pork ribs to the preheated Air Fryer and cook for 25 minutes at 370 degrees F.

Serve warm and top with the BBQ sauce. Enjoy!

Nutritional Information

Calories 576; Fat 35.1g; Carbs 12.5g; Fiber 1.7g; Protein 31.4g

18. Pork Schnitzel

3 Servings   15 minutes +
marinating time

Ingredients

- 3 boneless pork chops
- Salt and pepper, to taste
- 1/2 cup all-purpose flour
- ½ cup breadcrumbs
- 1 tablespoon honey
- 2 tablespoons olive oil
- 1 tablespoon Dijon mustard
- 1 tablespoon soy sauce

Directions

Place the pork chops together with the soy sauce, honey, olive oil, and Dijon mustard in a zip-top plastic bag. Seal and place in your refrigerator for 30 minutes

Remove the pork from the marinade and season with salt and pepper. Coat with flour and then dip it into the breadcrumbs.

Cook in the preheated Air Fryer at 370 degrees F for 12 minutes or until cooked through.

Serve warm. Bon appétit!

Nutritional Information

Calories 436; Fat 20.8g; Carbs 15.6g; Fiber 1.2g; Protein 35.5g

19. Pork Chops with Mushrooms

2 Servings   25 minutes

Ingredients

- 1 tablespoon olive oil
- ½ lb. pork chops
- 1/2 teaspoon dried oregano
- 1/4 teaspoon red pepper flakes
- 1 teaspoon dried thyme
- ½ teaspoon salt
- ½ teaspoon pepper
- 6 large mushrooms, cleaned and sliced
- 1 large yellow onion, chopped
- 1 ½ tablespoons soy sauce
- 2 tablespoons fresh parsley, finely chopped

Directions

Place the pork chops, onion, mushrooms, salt, pepper, thyme, soy sauce, oregano, red pepper flakes, and olive oil into a large bowl and mix.

Transfer the pork chops and mushrooms to the preheated Air Fryer at 390 degrees F for 20 minutes.

Serve warm and sprinkle with fresh parsley. Bon appétit!

Nutritional Information

Calories 233; Fat 11.2g; Carbs 5.7g; Fiber 1.4g; Protein 27.7g

20. Pork Sausages with Mustard Sauce

2 Servings   25 minutes

Ingredients

- 4 pork sausages
- Non-stick cooking spray
- **For the Mustard sauce:**
- 1 tablespoon mayonnaise
- ½ cup Dijon mustard
- 1 tablespoon honey

Directions

Prick holes in the sausages.

Then, transfer the sausages to the preheated Air Fryer and cook for 18 minutes at 370 degrees F.

Meanwhile, in a small bowl mix the mayonnaise, honey, and Dijon mustard. Combine well.

Serve the warm sausages topped with the mustard sauce. Bon appétit!

Nutritional Information

Calories 501; Fat 34.4g; Carbs 2.1g; Fiber 0.1g; Protein 44.8g

21. Spaghetti with Beef Meatballs

3 Servings   20 minutes

Ingredients

- 1 ½ cup ground beef
- ½ yellow onion, chopped
- 5 tablespoons seasoned bread-crumbs
- 1/2 teaspoon cumin powder
- 1 ½ tablespoon fresh parsley, minced
- 1/2 teaspoon salt
- ¼ teaspoon pepper
- 1 package spaghetti pasta, cooked

Directions

Place the ground beef, yellow onion, and finely chopped parsley into a large bowl. Combine well. Stir in the breadcrumbs, cumin, salt, and pepper. Mix well.

Then, shape the mixture into small balls. Place the meatballs in the preheated Air Fryer at 370 degrees F for 12 minutes, shaking the basket halfway through the cooking time.

Serve the warm meatballs over the cooked spaghetti. Bon appétit!

Nutritional Information

Calories 484; Fat 13.6g; Carbs 45.5g; Fiber 5.6g; Protein 44.6g

22. Beef Cubes with Root Vegetables

4 Servings   20 minutes +
marinating time

Ingredients

- 1 lb. beef sirloin steak, cut into cubes
- 1/3 cup sesame oil
- ½ teaspoon salt
- 1/4 cup soy sauce
- 1/2 teaspoon pepper
- 1/2 teaspoon garlic powder
- 1/4 teaspoon ground cumin
- ¼ cup fresh lemon juice
- 1 teaspoon dried basil
- 1 tablespoon dried parsley
- 2 carrots, sliced
- 1 large onion, sliced
- 2 Russet potatoes, peeled and sliced
- 1 ½ tablespoon fresh coriander, finely chopped

Directions

In a large bowl add the beef cubes, sesame oil, lemon juice, salt, pepper, garlic powder, soy sauce, cumin, basil, and parsley. Coat well and refrigerate for 2 hours.

Place the beef cubes, carrots, onion, and potatoes in the preheated Air Fryer. Cook at 360 degrees F for 20 minutes or until cooked through.

Serve immediately. Bon appétit!

Nutritional Information

Calories 444; Fat 17.5g; Carbs 43.2g; Fiber 3.7g; Protein 28.5g

23. Spring Style Flank Steak

4 Servings 15 minutes + marinating time

Ingredients

- 1 1/2 lb. flank steak
- 1 teaspoon salt
- ½ teaspoon pepper
- 2 tablespoons fresh thyme, chopped
- 2 teaspoons honey
- 3 garlic cloves, minced
- 1 ½ teaspoon paprika
- 1 ½ tablespoon fresh rosemary, finely chopped
- 4 tablespoons olive oil

Directions

Add the olive oil, salt, pepper, flank steak, honey, thyme, paprika, garlic, and rosemary in a sealable food bag. Shake until completely coated and refrigerate for at least 2 hours.

Then, place the steak in the preheated Air Fryer. Cook at 390 degrees F for 15 minutes, flipping once.

Serve immediately. Bon appétit!

Nutritional Information

Calories 253; Fat 8.5g; Carbs 4.5g; Fiber 0.6g; Protein 36.4g

24. Holiday Beef Tenderloin

4 Servings

20 minutes

Ingredients

- 4 beef tenderloin steaks
- Salt and pepper, to your taste
- 1 teaspoon dried oregano
- 1 teaspoon dried thyme
- 1 teaspoon marjoram
- 1 teaspoon dried sage
- 1 teaspoon garlic powder
- 1 teaspoon dried coriander
- 2 tablespoons olive oil
- 2 eggs, well-whisked
- 1/2 cup seasoned breadcrumbs

Directions

In a large bowl mix the olive oil, salt, pepper, thyme, oregano, sage, marjoram, garlic powder, oregano, and coriander.

Season the beef steaks with the prepared herb mixture.

Add the whisked egg to a shallow bowl. Place the breadcrumbs in another bowl.

Coat the beef tenderloin with the egg. Then, lay it into the breadcrumbs. Place the steaks in the preheated Air Fryer and cook at 380 degrees F for 11 minutes or until cooked through.

Serve with fresh salad and potatoes. Enjoy!

Nutritional Information

Calories 243; Fat 8.6g; Carbs 2.1g; Fiber 0.6g; Protein 38.4g

25. Special Beef Cheeseburgers

Ingredients

- ½ lb. ground beef
- 1/3 cup breadcrumbs
- 2 tablespoons parsley, finely chopped
- 3 tablespoons parmesan cheese, shredded
- ½ teaspoon salt
- 1/3 teaspoon pepper
- 4 slices Cheddar cheese
- 4 burger buns
- 1 red onion, sliced
- 4 romaine lettuce leaves
- 4 teaspoons mayonnaise
- 1cup pickles, sliced

Directions

In a mixing dish, combine the ground beef, salt, pepper, breadcrumbs, parmesan cheese, and parsley. Mix well.

Shape the mixture into 4 patties and place them in your preheated Air Fryer. Cook at 390 degrees F for 13 minutes.

Then, place the cheese slices on top of the warm burgers and Air fry for one more minute.

Serve on burger buns and top with pickles, red onion, lettuce leaves, and mayonnaise. Enjoy!

Nutritional Information

Calories 401; Fat 22.2g; Carbs 16.5g; Fiber 1.8g; Protein 20.1g

26. Glazed Cod Fillets

4 Servings   15 minutes

Ingredients

- 4 cod fillets
- Salt and pepper, to taste
- 1 teaspoon mirin
- 2 tablespoons honey
- 1/4 cup vegetable oil
- 1 ½ tablespoons teriyaki sauce
- 1 tablespoon freshly squeezed lemon juice
- 1 teaspoon dried basil

Directions

In a large bowl, mix all of the ingredients. Stir well and coat the fish evenly.

Place the fish in the preheated Air Fryer basket and cook for 10 minutes at 380 degrees F or until cooked through.

Serve warm. Bon appétit!

Nutritional Information

Calories 394; Fat 14.1g; Carbs 10.2g; Fiber 0.1g; Protein 41.6g

27. Tasty Shrimps

2 Servings   35 minutes

Ingredients

- 1/2lb. shrimps, shelled and deveined
- 2 tablespoons freshly squeezed lemon juice
- 1/2 teaspoon paprika
- 1/2 teaspoon fine sea salt
- 2 tablespoons sesame oil
- 3 garlic cloves, peeled and minced
- 1 teaspoon onion powder
- 1/2 teaspoon dried oregano
- 1/2 cup fresh parsley, coarsely chopped

Directions

In a mixing dish add the lemon juice, salt, paprika, sesame oil, minced garlic, onion powder, oregano, parsley, and shrimps. Stir and cover. Let them marinate for 40 minutes in your refrigerator.

Then, place the shrimps in the preheated Air Fryer and cook for 6 minutes at 390 degrees F, turning them over once or twice to ensure even cooking.

Serve with your favorite salad and enjoy!

Nutritional Information

Calories 355; Fat 15.1g; Carbs 4.5g; Fiber 1.1g; Protein 51.2g

28. Flounder Fillets with Creamy-Mayo Sauce

4 Servings   15 minutes

Ingredients

- 4 flounder fillets
- 1 ½ tablespoon sesame oil
- Salt and pepper, to taste
- **For the Creamy-Mayo Sauce:**
- 1/2 cup crème fraîche
- 3 tablespoons mayonnaise
- 1/3 cup Parmesan cheese
- 2 tablespoons green onion, finely chopped

Directions

Drizzle the flounder fillets with sesame oil and season with salt and pepper.

Place the fillets in a single layer at the bottom of the preheated Air Fryer and cook at 370 degrees F for 12 minutes. Shake the basket halfway through the cooking time.

Meanwhile, in a bowl mix the mayonnaise, parmesan cheese, green onion, and crème fraiche.

Serve the flounder fillets and top with the mayo sauce. Bon appétit!

Nutritional Information

Calories 282; Fat 15.6g; Carbs 4.4g; Fiber 0.4g; Protein 29.8g

29. Salmon Fillets with Lemon Sauce

Ingredients

- 4 skin-on salmon fillets
- 2 tablespoons melted butter
- 1 teaspoon salt
- 1/2 teaspoon pepper
- ½ teaspoon dried marjoram
- ½ teaspoon dried oregano
- ½ teaspoon dried thyme
- 1 ½ tablespoon lemon juice
- 4 lemon slices

Directions

Brush the salmon fillets with butter and lemon juice on all sides. Season with salt, pepper, marjoram, oregano, and thyme.

Place the salmon fillets in the preheated Air Fryer basket and arrange the lemon slices on top of the fillets. Cook at 390 degrees F for 11 or until cooked through.

Serve immediately. Bon appétit!

Nutritional Information

Calories 459; Fat 19.7g; Carbs 0.2g; Fiber 0.3g; Protein 65.4g

30. Crispy Fish Fillets with Tartar Sauce

4 Servings   20 minutes

Ingredients

- 1 cup breadcrumbs
- 1/3 cup vegetable oil
- 1 teaspoon garlic powder
- 1/2 teaspoon onion powder
- 2 eggs, well whisked
- 4 cod fish fillets
- Salt and pepper, to taste
- ½ teaspoon paprika
- **For the Tartar Sauce:**
- 1 cup mayonnaise
- 1 teaspoon Dijon mustard
- 1 1/2 tablespoon fresh dill, finely chopped
- 1 ½ tablespoon fresh lemon juice
- ½ teaspoon Worcestershire sauce
- ½ teaspoon salt
- ½ teaspoon pepper

Directions

In a bowl combine well the paprika, breadcrumbs, and vegetable oil.

In another bowl, combine the whisked egg, garlic powder, and onion powder. Season the fish fillets with salt and pepper.

Dip each fillet into the beaten egg. Then, coat the fillets in the crumb mixture.

Place the fillets in the preheated Air Fryer at 390 degrees F and cook for 12 minutes.

Meanwhile, in a mixing bowl add all ingredients for the Tartar sauce. Combine well.

Serve the warm fish and top with the Tartar sauce. Enjoy!

Nutritional Information

Calories 491; Fat 30.3g; Carbs 7.6g; Fiber 2.4g; Protein 25.2g

31. Colorful Vegetable Skewers

5 Servings   20 minutes

Ingredients

- 1 zucchini, cut into circles
- 1 teaspoon wholegrain mustard
- 5 cherry tomatoes
- 2 carrots, sliced into circles
- 1 red bell pepper, sliced into chunks
- 2 cloves garlic, minced
- 1 red onion, cut into wedges
- 1/4 cup olive oil
- 1/2 teaspoon salt
- 1/2 teaspoon pepper
- 1 teaspoon dried basil
- ½ teaspoon dried oregano
- 10 small mushrooms

Directions

In a large mixing bowl place all of the ingredients and mix well. Then thread the vegetables onto bamboo skewers.

Cook in the preheated Air Fryer for 12 minutes at 390 degrees F, turning them over once or twice to ensure even cooking.

Serve immediately. Bon appétit!

Nutritional Information

Calories 157; Fat 13.8g; Carbs 8.2g; Fiber 1.6g; Protein 1.8g

32. Potatoes with Tahini-Mustard Sauce

3 Servings   30 minutes

Ingredients

- 6 Russet potatoes, cut into wedges
- 1 teaspoon sesame oil
- 1/2 teaspoon salt
- 1/3 teaspoon red pepper flakes, crushed
- For the Tahini-Mustard Sauce:
- 2 ½ tablespoons yellow mustard
- 1/3 teaspoon salt
- 1 teaspoon dried oregano
- 1 teaspoon lemon juice
- 1/3 cup tahini dressing
- 1 tablespoon water

Directions

In a large bowl toss the potatoes with sesame oil, salt, and red pepper flakes.

Add the potatoes to the preheated Air Fryer and cook them at 390 degrees F for 22 minutes or until cooked through.

Then, thoroughly combine all the ingredients for the mustard sauce and mix well.

Serve the warm potatoes with the tahini-mustard sauce and enjoy!

Nutritional Information

Calories 350; Fat 1.8g; Carbs 70g; Fiber 5.5g; Protein 9.1g

33. Carrot Sticks with Vegan Mayonnaise

 2 Servings 15 minutes

Ingredients

- 6 carrots, washed, debris removed and sliced lengthways
- ½ teaspoon salt
- 1/2 teaspoon pepper
- 1/4 teaspoon dried dill weed
- 1 tablespoon olive oil
- ½ cup vegan mayonnaise
- 1 teaspoon lemon juice
- ½ teaspoon garlic powder

Directions

In a bowl add the carrots, salt, pepper, dill, and olive oil. Mix well.

Place the carrots in the preheated Air Fryer and cook them at 380 degrees F for 11 minutes. turning them over once or twice to ensure even cooking.

Meanwhile, in a small bowl mix the lemon juice, garlic powder, and vegan mayonnaise. Stir well.

Serve warm with the vegan mayonnaise dipping. Bon appétit!

Nutritional Information

Calories 498; Fat 17.2g; Carbs 8.5; Fiber 0.3g; Protein 38.6g

34. Herb-Roasted Sweet Potatoes

3 Servings | 30 minutes

Ingredients

- 5 Sweet potatoes, peeled and cut into wedges
- 1 ½ tablespoon sesame oil
- 2 tablespoons fresh thyme, chopped
- 1 sprig rosemary, chopped
- 1/3 teaspoon Italian seasoning
- ½ cup parmesan cheese, shredded

Directions

In a large bowl add the sesame oil, sweet potatoes, fresh thyme, rosemary, and Italian seasoning. Mix well.

Place the potatoes in the preheated Air Fryer and cook them at 380 degrees F for 24 minutes. Shake the basket halfway through the cooking time.

Serve warm and top with parmesan cheese.

Nutritional Information

Calories 319; Fat 11.5g; Carbs 46.6g; Fiber 6.4g; Protein 8.6g

35. Crispy Asparagus with Vegan Cream Sauce

 2 Servings   15 minutes

Ingredients

- 1 tablespoon olive oil
- ½ lb. asparagus, chopped
- ½ teaspoon pepper
- ½ teaspoon salt
- For the Creamy Sauce:
- 1 large garlic clove, minced
- 1 tablespoon sesame oil
- ½ tablespoon flour
- ½ cup almond milk
- ½ teaspoon turmeric
- 1/3 teaspoon salt
- 1/3 teaspoon pepper

Directions

In a large bowl mix the asparagus, salt, pepper, and olive oil.

Then, place the asparagus in the preheated Air Fryer and cook them at 380 degrees F for 5 minutes.

Meanwhile, in a saucepan preheat the sesame oil. Add the garlic and sauté until aromatic. Stir in the flour and whisk for 1 minute. Then, add the milk, salt, pepper, and turmeric. Simmer until a thick consistency is reached.

Serve the warm asparagus topped with the sauce. Enjoy!

Nutritional Information

Calories 145; Fat 6.9g; Carbs 5.4g; Fiber 2.6g; Protein 2.6g

36. Homemade Apple Chips

3 Servings   15 minutes

Ingredients

- 3 medium apples, washed, cored, and thinly sliced
- Non-stick cooking spray
- 1/2 cup freshly squeezed lemon juice
- 1 teaspoon cinnamon
- 2 tablespoons avocado oil

Directions

Lightly coat the apples with avocado oil and lemon juice.

Place the slices in the preheated Air Fryer at 200 degrees F for 8 minutes, turning them over once or twice to ensure even cooking. Work in batches.

Take the apple slices out of the Air Fryer. Sprinkle with cinnamon and store them in an airtight container. Enjoy!

Nutritional Information

Calories 189; Fat 9.8g; Carbs 28.6; Fiber 5g; Protein 0.6g

37. Parmesan Corn with Coriander

2 Servings   15 minutes

Ingredients

- 2 ears corn, husked and cleaned
- 1 tablespoon melted butter
- 1 tablespoon fresh coriander, finely chopped
- 2 tablespoons parmesan cheese, finely chopped

Directions

Rub the corn with the butter. Then, arrange the corn in the preheated Air Fryer and cook for 14 minutes at 400 degrees F or until cooked through.

Serve warm and top with fresh coriander and parmesan cheese. Bon appétit!

Nutritional Information

Calories 195; Fat 9g; Carbs 27.4; Fiber 2.9g; Protein 6.2g

38. Mini Sausages with Dijon Dip

4 Servings   20 minutes

Ingredients

- 1/2 lb. cocktail sausages
- **For the Dijon Dip:**
- 4 tablespoons mayonnaise
- 2 tablespoons Dijon mustard
- 1 ½ tablespoon honey
- 1 teaspoon lemon juice
- ¼ teaspoon pepper

Directions

Using a fork, give your sausages a few pricks.

Place them in the preheated Air Fryer at 390 degrees F for 17 minutes, shaking the basket halfway through the cooking time.

Then, in a bowl mix all the ingredients for the Dijon dip.

Serve the warm sausages with the mustard dip on the side. Enjoy!

Nutritional Information

Calories 448; Fat 30g; Carbs 26.6; Fiber 4.3g; Protein 23.5g

39. Chicken Drumsticks with BBQ Sauce

5 Servings   20 minutes

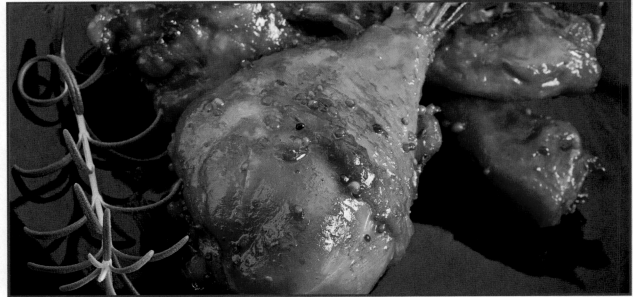

Ingredients

- **For the Sauce:**
- 1 tablespoon Worcestershire sauce
- 1 tablespoon red wine vinegar
- 1 tablespoon olive oil
- 1 ½ cup ketchup
- 1 tablespoon mustard
- 1 tablespoon brown sugar
- 1 tablespoon honey
- ½ teaspoon granulated garlic
- Salt and pepper, to taste
- 1/8 teaspoon ground allspice
- 1/4 cup water
- **For the Chicken Drumsticks:**
- 2 lb. chicken drumsticks
- 1/3 teaspoon Kosher salt
- 1/3 cup fresh parsley, finely chopped

Directions

In a sauté pan over a medium-high flame, add all the sauce ingredients and let them simmer. Then, reduce the temperature and cook until it thickens.

Meanwhile, preheat your Air Fryer to 390 degrees F and cook the chicken drumsticks for 15 minutes or until cooked through. Finally, season them with Kosher salt.

Serve warm with the prepared sauce and top with finely chopped parsley. Bon appétit!

Nutritional Information

Calories 279; Fat 10.4g; Carbs 7.1; Fiber 0.5g; Protein 38g

40. Healthy Cauliflower Appetizer

2 Servings   20 minutes

Ingredients

- 5 cup cauliflower florets
- ½ teaspoon Kosher salt
- 1/2 teaspoon paprika
- ½ teaspoon garlic powder
- 2 tablespoons avocado oil

Directions

In a large bowl add the avocado oil, salt, paprika, garlic powder, and cauliflower florets. Coat well.

Then, place the cauliflower in the preheated Air Fryer basket and cook at 390 degrees for 18 minutes. Shake the basket halfway through the cooking time. Work in batches.

Serve immediately. Bon appétit!

Nutritional Information

Calories 164; Fat 11.3g; Carbs 14.2; Fiber 5.3g; Protein 5.3g

41. Scrambled Eggs with Bacon and Green Onion

2 Servings 10 minutes

Ingredients

- 4 eggs, whisked
- 1 teaspoon fresh lemon juice
- 1 ½ tablespoons butter, melted
- 1/3 cup mozzarella cheese, shredded
- ½ cup bacon, diced
- 1/2 teaspoon salt
- 1 tablespoon fresh chives, finely chopped
- 1/2 teaspoon pepper

Directions

In a bowl add the eggs, salt, and pepper. Whisk well. Then, stir in the bacon, mozzarella, and lemon juice.

Add an Air Fryer compatible baking pan in your Air Fryer's basket.

Add the melted butter to the preheated Air Fryer baking pan and pour the egg mixture.

Cook for 4 minutes at 290 degrees F or until the eggs are set. Serve immediately and garnish with the fresh chive. Enjoy!

Nutritional Information

Calories 247; Fat 17.2g; Carbs 4.3g; Fiber 1g; Protein 18.9g

42. Quick Potato Balls

Ingredients

- 2 cups mashed potatoes
- ½ teaspoon salt
- 1 teaspoon cumin
- 1/4 teaspoon paprika
- 1/2 cup shallots, chopped
- 2 cloves garlic, minced
- 1 ½ tablespoon fresh chopped parsley
- 1 egg, whisked
- 3/4 cup Colby cheese, grated
- ¼ cup breadcrumbs

Directions

In a large mixing bowl add all the ingredients and mix well. Shape balls from the mixture.

Then, spritz the balls with cooking spray. Place them in a single layer in your preheated Air Fryer at 350 degrees F for 10 minutes. Shake the basket halfway through the cooking time and work in batches.

Serve warm and enjoy!

Nutritional Information

Calories 406; Fat 21.1g; Carbs 35.2; Fiber 3.3g; Protein 19.5g

43. Italian-Style Veggies

3 Servings 20 minutes

Ingredients

- 1 eggplant, peeled and cut into cubes
- 1 zucchini, cut into cubes
- 10 cherry tomatoes, halved
- ½ teaspoon salt
- ½ teaspoon pepper
- 1 large red bell pepper, seeded and sliced
- 1/4 cup canola oil
- 1 teaspoon dried oregano
- 1 yellow onion, sliced
- ½ tablespoon apple cider vinegar
- 2 tablespoons white wine

Directions

Toss the eggplant, yellow pepper, zucchini, onion, and tomato in a large bowl.

Drizzle with canola oil, vinegar, and white wine. Season with salt, pepper, oregano, and basil. Combine well.

Then, place the vegetables in the preheated Air Fryer at 390 degrees F for 15 minutes or until cooked through.

Serve warm and enjoy!

Nutritional Information

Calories 245; Fat 18.3g; Carbs 19.1g; Fiber 7.2g; Protein 3.9g

44. Easy Air-Fried Zucchini

2 Servings   15 minutes

Ingredients

- 7 zucchinis, peeled and thinly sliced
- 1/2 teaspoon salt
- 1/3 cup olive oil
- 1 teaspoon garlic powder
- 1 tablespoon dried rosemary
- 1/2 teaspoon dried dill weed
- 1/2 teaspoon pepper

Directions

In a large bowl toss the zucchini slices with oil, salt, garlic powder, rosemary, dill, and pepper.

Transfer them to the preheated Air Fryer and cook at 390 degrees F for 10 minutes. Work in batches.

Serve with your favorite sauce. Bon appétit!

Nutritional Information

Calories 331; Fat 18g; Carbs 36.7; Fiber 0.3g; Protein 6g

45. Egg Cups with Ham

4 Servings   15 minutes

Ingredients

- 1/4 cup spring onions, finely chopped
- 6 eggs, whisked
- ¼ teaspoon salt
- ¼ teaspoon pepper
- 1 cup cheddar cheese, shredded
- ½ cup ham, finely chopped

Directions

In a large bowl add all of the above ingredients and mix well.

Lightly oil a mini muffin pan (that fits in your Air Fryer) using cooking spray and divide the mixture among the muffin cups.

Bake in the preheated Air Fryer at 350 degrees F for 10 minutes or until cooked through.

Serve warm! Bon appétit!

Nutritional Information

Calories 174; Fat 11.8g; Carbs 3.7; Fiber 0.7g; Protein 12.9g

46. Aromatic Fried Banana

3 Servings 5 minutes

Ingredients

- 2 tablespoons coconut oil
- 5 tablespoons brown sugar
- 1/2 teaspoon cinnamon powder
- 3 ripe bananas, peeled and halved
- 1/3 cup almonds, finely chopped

Directions

In a small bowl mix the brown sugar and vanilla. Set aside.

Mist the bananas with coconut oil. Then cook the bananas in the preheated Air Fryer for 2 minutes at 390 degrees F.

Sprinkle the sugar mixture over the banana and cook for 1 minute more.

Serve warm and garnish with almonds and a dollop of vanilla ice cream. Enjoy!

Nutritional Information

Calories 274; Fat 14.5; Carbs 37.4g; Fiber 4.6g; Protein 3.6g

47. Marvelous Brownie with Dark Chocolate

4 Servings   20 minutes

Ingredients

- 1/3 cup butter, melted
- 1/3 cup dark chocolate, melted
- 1/2 cup sugar
- 2 tablespoons water
- 3 eggs, whisked
- 1/3 teaspoon salt
- ½ teaspoon baking powder
- 1/2 teaspoon vanilla extract
- 1/2 cup flour
- 1 cup fresh raspberries
- 1/3 cup cocoa powder

Directions

In a large bowl mix the butter, melted chocolate, water, eggs, salt, vanilla, and baking powder. Stir well.

After that, stir in the flour and coconut powder. Combine well. Then, press the mixture into a lightly buttered baking dish (that fits in your Air Fryer).

Bake in the preheated Air Fryer at 350 degrees F for 15 minutes.

Let your brownie cool and carefully remove it from the baking dish. Cut into squares and serve.

Garnish with the fresh raspberries and enjoy!

Nutritional Information

Calories 522; Fat 33.5g; Carbs 54.8; Fiber 6.4g; Protein 12.7g

48. Pears with Walnuts and Cranberries

3 Servings   15 minutes

Ingredients

- 3 pears, cored and halved
- 4 tablespoons honey
- 1 teaspoon ground cinnamon
- 1 teaspoon vanilla extract
- 1/4 cup walnuts, crushed
- 1/3 cup fresh cranberries

Directions

In a mixing bowl add the cinnamon, walnuts, and vanilla. Stir well.

Add the walnut mixture into the centers of the pears. Then, drizzle honey over each pear.

Arrange the pears in the basket of the Air Fryer.

Bake in the preheated Air Fryer at 350 degrees F for 10 minutes or until the topping is golden brown.

Serve warm and top with fresh cranberries.

Nutritional Information

Calories 305; Fat 12g; Carbs 48.8g; Fiber 6.5g; Protein 2.1g

49. Simple Strawberry Puff Pastries

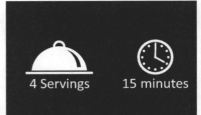

4 Servings | 15 minutes

Ingredients

- 1 package crescent dinner rolls, refrigerated
- 1/4 cup powdered sugar
- 1 cup strawberry jam
- 1 egg, whisked

Directions

Unroll the crescent dinner rolls and cut them into 6 squares. Then, divide the strawberry jam among the pastry squares.

Fold the dough over the filling, pressing the edges to help them seal well. Brush each pastry puff with the whisked egg.

Place in the preheated Air Fryer and cook for 9 minutes at 360 degrees F. Serve and enjoy!

Nutritional Information

Calories 270; Fat 8.4; Carbs 36.2g; Fiber 6.5g; Protein 12.1g

50. Banana Muffins with Walnuts

4 Servings | 20 minutes

Ingredients

- 5 tablespoons all-purpose flour
- 1/2 teaspoon baking powder
- 1/4 cup oats
- A pinch of salt
- 2 eggs, whisked
- 1/4 cup butter, melted
- 1/4 cup brown sugar
- 2 tablespoons banana puree
- 2 tablespoons walnuts, finely chopped
- 1/3 teaspoon vanilla
- 1/4 teaspoon ground cinnamon

Directions

In a bowl mix the flour, baking powder, salt, and oats. Stir well and set aside.

In another bowl add the whisked eggs, brown, sugar, banana puree, vanilla, cinnamon, and walnuts. Stir.

Then, add the egg mixture to the flour mixture. Combine well with a spatula.

Prepare muffin molds and add muffin liners to each of them. Divide the mixture between the molds.

Bake in preheated Air Fryer at 330 degrees F for 15 minutes. Leave them to cool and remove from the molds. Bon appétit!

Nutritional Information

Calories 386; Fat 15.6g; Carbs 54.1; Fiber 4.6g; Protein 9.8g

Made in the USA
Middletown, DE
02 November 2022

13951461R00031